Grand Bund

10/18 8/10/

21.29

EXPLORING THE
ANCIENT MAYA

by Elaine A. Kule

12 STORY LIBRARY

www.12StoryLibrary.com

12-Story Library is an imprint of Bookstaves and Press Room Editions

Produced for 12-Story Library by Red Line Editorial

Photographs ©: Rafal Cichawa/Shutterstock Images, cover, 1; Rainer Lesniewski/Shutterstock Images, 4; haydukepdx/iStockphoto, 5; Pedre/iStockphoto, 6; Los Angeles County Museum of Art, 7, 16, 26; gionnixxx/iStockphoto, 8, 29; North Wind Picture Archives, 9, 15, 28; Anton_Ivanov/Shutterstock Images, 10; Avi_Cohen_Nehemia/iStockphoto, 11; ART Collection/Alamy, 12; Septemberlegs/Alamy, 13; ChrisVanLennepPhoto/iStockphoto, 14; Diego Grandi/Shutterstock Images, 17; SmileKorn/Shutterstock Images, 18; chang/iStockphoto, 19; Leeuwtje/iStockphoto, 20; diegograndi/iStockphoto, 21; CampPhoto/iStockphoto, 22; gsermek/iStockphoto, 23; SimonDannhauer/iStockphoto, 24; The British Library, 25; Marlon Gomez/LatinContent/Getty Images, 27

Content Consultant: Jon B. Hageman, Professor of Anthropology, Northeastern Illinois University

Library of Congress Cataloging-in-Publication Data
Names: Kule, Elaine A., author.
Title: Exploring the Ancient Maya / by Elaine A. Kule.
Description: Mankato, MN : 12 Story Library, an imprint of Bookstaves and
  Press Room Editions, 2018. | Series: Exploring Ancient Civilizations |
  Includes bibliographical references and index. | Audience: Grades 4 to 6.
Identifiers: LCCN 2016047631 (print) | LCCN 2016047930 (ebook) | ISBN
  9781632354655 (hardcover : alk. paper) | ISBN 9781632355300 (pbk. : alk.
  paper) | ISBN 9781621435822 (hosted e-book)
Subjects: LCSH: Mayas--Social life and customs--Juvenile literature. |
  Mayas--Civilization--Juvenile literature. | Mayas--History--Juvenile
  literature.
Classification: LCC F1435.3.S7 K85 2018 (print) | LCC F1435.3.S7 (ebook) |
  DDC 972.81--dc23
LC record available at https://lccn.loc.gov/2016047631

Printed in the United States of America
022017

Access free, up-to-date content on this topic plus a full digital version of this book. Scan the QR code on page 31 or use your school's login at 12StoryLibrary.com.

Table of Contents

The Ancient Maya Built a Civilization

The ancient Maya lived in Mexico and Central America. Today, modern Maya descendants still live there. They carry on some traditions from ancient times.

The Maya civilization began around 2500 BCE. Earlier, people in the area were hunters and gatherers. People made axes and other tools from stone. They cut down trees to clear land. They built huts. Most became farmers.

They grew cotton for clothing. They planted maize. Other crops were beans and squash. The Maya caught fish in nets. They hunted animals using bows and arrows. They learned to make pottery. Traders packed their goods

Modern Maya people live in Mexico, Guatemala, Belize, and other Central American countries.

MEXICO

Gulf of Mexico

BELIZE

GUATEMALA

HONDURAS

PACIFIC OCEAN

EL SALVADOR

NICARAGUA

The ruins of Mayapan

in canoes. They traveled throughout the region.

The Maya set up villages by around 1000 BCE. Many villages grew into cities. Each city had its own government. Rulers controlled everyone in their city-states. The name Maya comes from one city, Mayapan. The Maya people refer to themselves by many names, depending on their language and where they live.

30

Number of Mayan languages spoken today.

- The ancient Maya lived in Central America and Mexico.
- Maya descendants still live there and follow some ancient traditions.
- Most ancient Maya were farmers, growing maize, beans, and squash.
- Each Maya city had its own government and ruler.

THINK ABOUT IT

The ancient Maya were not the only people to thrive in Mexico and Central America. Do a little research to find out more about these other civilizations. Why do you think so many people thrived in this region?

Ancient Maya Culture Developed through Trading

The Maya developed near several other advanced civilizations. Experts believe that trading with other groups may have helped the ancient Maya develop their culture. One group, the Olmec, likely had a big effect on the Maya. The Olmec lived in Mexico. Their civilization lasted from around 1500 BCE to 400 BCE. They exchanged pottery with the Maya. Both peoples admired a green stone called jade. Both planted maize and made books using folded pages. Both wrote using hieroglyphics. The Maya, however, used pictures to represent sounds.

Jaguar carvings are common on Maya temples, as well as temples from many other civilizations in Mexico.

Historians divide the Maya civilization into three major periods. The Preclassic ran from 2500 BCE to 300 CE. Maya cities gained power and traded with one another and with distant neighbors. They developed mathematics, calendars, and writing. Artisans began carving stone stelae, or columns, and altars.

In the Classic period (300–800 CE), the Maya people built epic monuments. Pyramids seemed to touch the sky. Priests performed rituals to many gods. But the quickly growing population may have caused cities to compete. War spread by the 600s. Changing climate likely played a role, too. A long period of drought made farming difficult. Many cities were abandoned by the 800s. The remaining important cities formed shifting alliances and battled one another. This Postclassic period starting in the 800s lasted until Spanish soldiers arrived in 1502 and overthrew native rule.

1 million
Maya population in the region of modern Belize around 600 CE.

- Trading with the Olmec civilization may have helped develop the Maya culture.
- Maya cities traded with one another and with distant neighbors during the Preclassic period.
- Maya cities reached their height during the Classic period with a high population and epic monuments.
- Maya cities declined in the Postclassic period until the Spanish conquest of the region.

Ancient Maya Rulers Led City-States

There was never a Maya emperor. Instead, Maya city-states were led by different rulers. No city ever ruled over all the others. City-state rulers were usually sons who took over the position from their fathers. Women took over if there was not a male in the family. For example, the city-state of Palenque had its first queen in 583 CE. Lady Yohl Ik'nal ruled the lowland city until her death in 604 CE.

Rulers lived in elegant palaces. They wore feathered headdresses and jade necklaces. Everyone honored them. Farmers shared their harvests. Traders brought their goods. Others offered their handiwork, such as art, pottery, or cloth. Laborers worked on large public building projects.

The city-state of Palenque was at its height from 500 to 700 CE.

12

Age of King K'inich Janaab' Pakal when he began his 68-year rule of Palenque in 615 CE.

- There was never one Maya nation.
- Rulers usually received their positions through their families.
- People honored their rulers with food, goods, and services.
- There were many wars between the city-states.

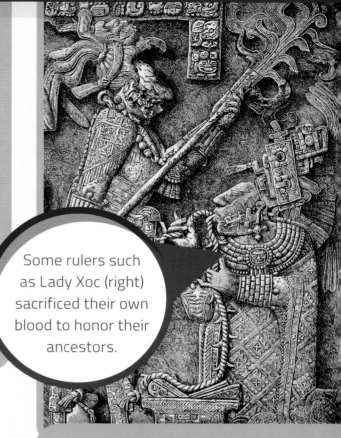

Some rulers such as Lady Xoc (right) sacrificed their own blood to honor their ancestors.

Maya rulers often declared war on other city-states. They waited until after a harvest. One reason for war was to capture enemies. Capturing soldiers weakened the other army. The captives could become slaves. Some were killed in sacrifice to the gods. Another purpose was to win farming land. The right to control a good trade route led to fighting as well. For example, the city-state of Naranjo had rich soil. The settlement was situated between two rivers. Naranjo's neighbors often attacked the city-state. It rarely had peace.

WOMEN WHO RULED

Tikal was one of the largest city-states in the lowlands. Lady of Tikal became its queen in 511 CE. She was six years old. An army general helped her lead. She may have ruled until 527 CE. In Naranjo, Lady Six Sky married the king in 682 CE. He named her the city's leader before he died. She successfully led battles against a neighboring enemy.

The Ancient Maya Worshipped Many Gods

The Maya prayed to gods and goddesses. There were more than 250 of them. The Maya thought the gods and goddesses controlled every part of life. For example, the rain god made sure crops had enough water for plentiful harvests. The Maya also believed in a link between the moon goddess and water. They prayed to her, too. The moon's changes helped the Maya decide when to plant crops.

This carving from Copán may have been made to honor monkey gods.

The ancient Maya believed spiritual forces were everywhere. They thought their ancestors' spirits lived in mountains. Eclipses terrified the Maya. To them it meant a sky serpent was biting the sun or moon. The Maya disliked rainbows. They believed rainbows caused diseases.

The Maya believed their rulers were a link to the gods. Men built pyramids to honor their dead royalty. A pyramid is a large building. It has

Pyramid at the Maya city-state of Xunantunich

365
Number of steps on the El Castillo pyramid.

- The Maya believed their gods and goddesses controlled every part of life.
- The Maya believed their ancestors' spirits lived in mountains.
- Rainbows were bad luck and thought to cause disease.
- Pyramids honored dead royalty, who were a link to the gods.

a square base. Maya pyramids have sloping sides with large steps. The flat tops hold temples. Maya priests held prayer services there to honor their gods and ancestors. Temples also served as burial grounds for rulers.

11

The Ancient Maya Told Myths

The ancient Maya used myths to explain the world around them. Myths are often stories about the adventures of superhuman beings. These stories may also try to explain mysterious events. The Maya wrote about their myths.

They drew pictures of them on pottery and other artwork. One important source for these myths is the *Popol Vuh*. This book from Guatemala was written shortly after the Spanish came. The authors wanted to preserve Maya traditions and stories.

One story tells how the sun god and the sea god made the world. They began with rich soil. Then they made plants. They made lakes, rivers, and forests. They made animals. The sun god and sea god told the animals where to live. But the gods were disappointed that the creatures could not talk. The gods wanted beings that would honor them. So they decided to make people.

The gods tried making people out of mud. That did not work. Their words made no sense when they spoke.

This copy of the *Popol Vuh* from the early 1700s was written in Latin and Spanish.

They tried making them out of wood. Those beings could speak, but their hearts and minds were empty. Then they made eight people from maize. According to legend, the Maya are descended from these eight people. The story shows how important maize was to the ancient Maya.

There are other myths, too. Some are about the Hero Twins. They seem human but are more powerful. They enjoy fighting monsters. In one story, the Hero Twins battle Earthquake. The twins finally bury him. Earthquake's strength has held up Earth's mountains ever since. He can still be dangerous, though. People must be careful if Earthquake moves even a little.

1703
Year that a Spanish religious leader found the *Popol Vuh.*

- The Maya wrote and drew about their myths.
- One Maya legend is about how the gods made people out of maize.
- The Hero Twins appear in several myths.

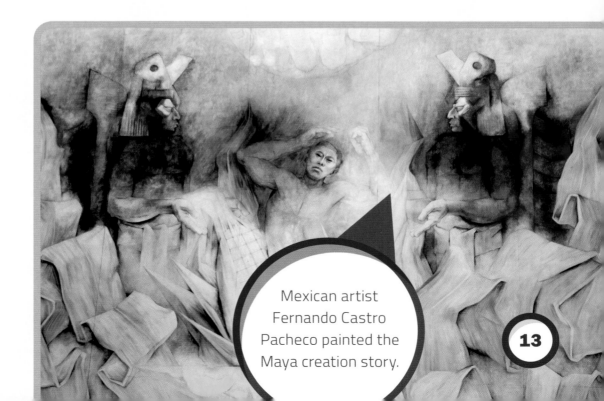

Mexican artist Fernando Castro Pacheco painted the Maya creation story.

13

Ancient Maya Families Were Close

Prayer was part of everyday life for the ancient Maya. People prayed for their children's good health. They asked their gods for successful harvests. Most Maya families worked the land. Men farmed and hunted wild game. They caught fish. Women worked in the family's garden. Tomatoes were among the vegetables grown there. Papaya and other fruits grew on nearby trees.

The ancient Maya gathered papaya fruit.

Mothers watched over their youngest children. They also made pottery. They wove cotton thread to make cloth. Older girls did chores. Boys worked with their fathers. Men helped one another build houses. Wooden poles supported the buildings. Roofs were made from woven palms. Some people strengthened the walls with a mixture of mud and straw. Other homes were made of stone.

Each family had a group of huts and an area of farmland. The huts surrounded a courtyard. One hut was for eating and sleeping. Another place was for cooking. Women made pottery in a different structure. They wove cotton there, too. There was usually a building for storing things. Families lived near one another. Many such family groups surrounded a city's public area. This city center had large buildings, plazas, and pyramids. It had markets where people traded.

There were class differences in Maya life. Royalty were in the highest group. Their helpers were

An ancient Maya woman spinning cotton

20
Average age when the ancient Maya married.

- Men farmed and hunted, and women cooked and gardened.
- The Maya built huts using wooden poles and palms.
- Farm families surrounded the city centers where the rulers and priests lived.
- Maya people were divided into classes.

below them. They all lived in or near the city's center. Writers and soldiers were in the middle class. Most farmers and traders were the lower class. They lived outside the city. Slaves were in the bottom group. Many came from very poor families. Others were enemy soldiers captured during wars. There were no schools for children. Most people could not read or write.

Customs Were Important to the Ancient Maya

When the ancient Maya moved from their homes, they smashed pottery. They left the broken pieces on the floors. Today some experts guess it was a cleansing ritual. Another custom was burying their dead loved ones under their homes. They placed food and a jade bead in their mouths. The bead might have been a symbol for the person's breath or spirit. In their graves were things the people used when they were alive. Burying ancestors under a home also proved that a family owned the land.

The ancient Maya began celebrating their New Year on the last five days of the old year. Special rituals were necessary so the world would not end. They built a clay statue. They brought it food. They prayed to it. Their services usually ended with music and dancing. The Maya used dance to express their spirituality. Some dancers wore costumes.

Beads placed in a dead loved one's mouth may have looked like this one.

MAYA MATS

The Maya used woven mats for sleeping. They thought sitting on mats gave them power. The mat was a sign of royalty. Kings and queens sat on a mat instead of a throne. The Maya sat on mats in gatherings to hear religious stories. The *Popol Vuh*, the book that tells of the Maya's creation, was called "The Book of the Mat."

They performed stories. Men and women rarely danced together.

Most people living in Mexico and Central America played a ritual ball game. The Maya played the ball game with two or more people. Players wore padding on their knees and arms. There were special courts with high walls. A stone hoop was at the top of each wall.

Players had to get the rubber ball through the hoop. But they could not use their hands. The person or team who got the ball through the hoop won the game. Sometimes the game was played for fun. Other times some players were sacrificed at the end of the game.

Players had to get the ball through the hoop, which was often several feet above the ground.

7.7
Maximum weight, in pounds (3.5 kg), of the rubber ball used in Maya ball games.

- The ancient Maya smashed pottery when they moved from their homes.
- They buried their dead loved ones under their homes.
- They built a clay statue before starting their new year.
- The Maya played a ball game for fun and for religious purposes.

17

Canoes Helped the Ancient Maya Become Active Traders

Canoes helped the ancient Maya travel. Some canoes held more than 25 people. They allowed people to exchange goods with one another. The Maya also traded with people living farther away. Cities near waterways, such as the Usumacinta River, Belize River, and Motagua River, became powerful.

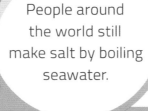

People around the world still make salt by boiling seawater.

JADE AND OBSIDIAN

The ancient Maya discovered jade in the highlands. Jade was prized because it was difficult to find. Artists made jewelry from it. It is a hard rock and difficult to cut. Rulers wore decorations made with jade. Obsidian is another rock from the highlands. It comes from volcanoes. The Maya used it to make sharp tools. Jade and obsidian were in demand throughout the region.

Humans need salt in order to live. And the Maya supplied lots of it. In city-states near the ocean, traders dammed up low-lying lagoons. The sun evaporated the water. Traders then collected the salt left behind and took it to other regions. Other people boiled seawater in pots.

Cacao beans were also important to traders. People enjoyed the chocolate drink made from them. The beans were precious because they did not keep well. Traders marketed pottery and jade, too. The Maya used cacao beans and beads made with jade as money.

Inside a cacao pod, cacao beans are covered in white pulp.

The Maya trade network stretched to distant lands. Shells from the coasts have been found inland. Large stones were shipped from the mountains. The Maya traded with people in Mexico and El Salvador. Gold and copper objects from the Postclassic period came from farther away. These objects show trade with Costa Rica and Columbia.

8
Width, in feet (2.4 m), of an ancient Maya canoe.

- Traders used canoes to travel throughout the region.
- They traded salt, cacao, jade, and pottery.
- The ancient Maya used cacao beans and beads made with jade as money.
- The Maya trade network stretched across Mexico and Central America.

19

The Ancient Maya Were Busy Inventors

The Maya developed their own way of writing using hieroglyphics. Their pictures represented sounds. They also made a special paper. The Maya folded the paper and made books. The books were about topics such as astronomy and farming.

The ancient Maya counted things based on groups of 20. Experts believe that figure came from the number of fingers and toes people have. The Maya wrote numbers using bars and dots. The bar represented five. A dot was one. They drew a shell for zero. The Maya were one of only a few ancient civilizations to use zero in calculations.

People throughout the region used calendars. The Maya had

0

Number the ancient Maya used to mark the first day in a month, instead of one.

- The Maya developed their own way of writing using hieroglyphics.
- They designed a way of counting based on groups of 20.
- They drew a shell to represent zero.
- They followed a system of several interlocking calendars.

This ancient Maya writing mentions the end of the 5,126-year cycle.

El Caracol in Chichén Itzá

an interlocking system of many calendars. The *Haab* calendar is 365 days and follows the sun. The *Tzolk'in* has 260 days. This calendar lines up with the moon's cycles. The Calendar Round is 52 years. This is how long it takes to make every combination of days in the *Haab* and *Tzolk'in* calendars. The new Calendar Round starts over on day one for both shorter calendars. The Long Count calendar keeps track of eras. It is 5,126 years long.

Maya scientists noted the changes of the sun and moon. They recorded the location of the planets. They built a high tower called El Caracol. It gave them a better view of the sky. It was especially helpful in tracking Venus. Scientists measured the changes of the sun during a solar eclipse. They measured the moon's changes during a lunar eclipse. They wrote what they saw in books.

ANCIENT PAPER

The Maya made a special paper. It came from the inner bark of fig trees. They soaked strips of the bark in a liquid mixture and then wove the strips together. They pounded the bark with a hammer until it was a flat sheet. The sheet was left to dry in the sun. Then it was smoothed with a rock. They covered the paper with plaster to make it even smoother.

The Ancient Maya Were Expert Farmers

Ninety percent of the Maya were involved in farming. The hard work of the ancient Maya fed more than 19 million people. They built stone canals. These helped supply water to those without rivers or springs nearby. The Maya collected rainwater in reservoirs.

Workers drained swamps. People made the swampland acceptable for farming. Some farmers built raised fields. These are large platforms of soil. The platforms protect crops from flooding. Terraces allowed farmers to grow crops on hillsides.

Many farmers used a method called *milpa*.

Some farmers in Guatemala still use terraces when farming.

10

Number of reservoirs in Tikal, a Maya city in Guatemala.

- The hard work of the ancient Maya fed millions of people.
- They successfully managed their water supply for many years.
- They used raised fields and terraces.
- The *milpa* method involved cutting and burning the forest.

Beans growing alongside corn

First they cut down a section of forest and burned it. Then they grew a series of crops for two years. After that, the farmers let the forest grow back for eight years. This system needs a lot of land. The farmers have to let the forest grow back, or the soil becomes less productive. Beans, squash, and maize were planted together. The beans grew up the maize stalks. The squash helped stop erosion. Maya cities without a lot of farmland traded other goods for food.

THINK ABOUT IT

People today still plant beans, maize, and squash together. These plantings are called three sisters gardens. Why do you think this idea is still being used?

The Ancient Maya Clashed with the Spanish

After approximately 800 CE, the Maya civilization started to change. The lowlands faced terrible droughts. Cutting down trees to create more farmland worsened the problem. The loss of trees caused a rise in temperature. It also brought less rainfall. Crops were ruined, causing a food shortage. People left the lowlands. Powerful cities such as Tikal, Caracol, and Calakmul were abandoned.

Wars in the highlands further weakened the Maya. Among the fighters was a group called the K'iche' Maya. They created a new kingdom in Guatemala that had new leaders. By 1200, the cities of Chichén Itzá, Mayapán, and Izamal had grown powerful in Mexico.

Contact with the Spanish began when Christopher Columbus visited the area in 1502. By this time, most Maya lived in villages. Monument building

Tikal is now a national park in Guatemala.

BOOK BURNING

Spain's spiritual leaders disliked the beliefs of the ancient Maya. They insisted on changing their culture. They burned their books. They thought they contained wrong ideas. They stopped the Maya from using hieroglyphics. The Maya learned Spanish and began writing in that language.

had stopped. Other explorers followed. They brought diseases to the area. Many Maya died. Spanish warriors heard there was gold in the region. They traveled there and demanded it from the Maya. They received some but wanted more. War broke out in 1524. The Spanish army destroyed the last ancient Maya city in 1697. But the Maya people survived. Today more than five million people speak Mayan languages and practice aspects of Maya culture in Mexico and Central America.

4

Number of books written by the ancient Maya that survived the Spanish book burning.

- Droughts started the end of the ancient Maya civilization.
- Clearing the land of trees worsened the drought.
- Ruined crops brought a food shortage.
- Disease and wars ended the ancient Maya civilization.

Signs.	Phonetic value.		Signs.	Phonetic value.		Signs.	Phonetic value.
	a		10.	i		19.	p
	a		11.	ca		20.	pp
	a		12.	k		21.	cu
	b		13.	l		22.	ku
	b		14.	l		23.	x#
	e		15.	m		24.	x
	t		16.	n		25.	u
	é		17.	o.		26.	u
						27.	z

Some Spanish priests tried to document the Mayan language.

25

The Ancient Maya Left Many Treasures

After some of the Maya city-states were abandoned, trees and plants began to take over. The buildings and structures remained undisturbed for hundreds of years. Then in the 1830s, an American explorer heard rumors of an ancient civilization in Central America. John Lloyd Stephens found several Maya ruins and wrote books about his findings. There have been many other visits to the area since then. Archaeologists unearthed countless treasures.

Among them were vases, plates, and bowls. Other findings were jade, pearls, and turquoise.

Experts have studied the ancient Maya to learn more about their civilization. Language

This painting of the maize god was made during the Classic period.

THINK ABOUT IT

Many tourists visit ancient Maya ruins every day. But walking on and touching these ruins can damage them. What are the pros and cons of making ancient ruins available only to archaeologists?

3,500
Minimum number of tourists who visit the ruins of Chichén Itzá every day.

- Maya cities laid undisturbed in the forest for centuries.
- Archaeologists have found art and stone monuments.
- Maya writing tells the people's history.
- Today the Maya mix modern with ancient ways of life.

Actors recreate the ancient Maya ball game for tourists in Guatemala.

Pottery from the ancient Maya has lasted for centuries.

specialist Yuri Knorosov realized in 1952 that Maya hieroglyphics represent speech sounds. His discovery helped others understand Maya writings. Many Maya stone monuments and stelae survive. Their carvings tell Maya history.

Many of today's Maya mix ancient and modern ways of life. They speak Mayan languages alongside Spanish. Some practice Christianity mixed with their traditional religion. Many farm maize and beans using hand tools as their ancestors did. Villages have public spaces surrounded by farms, much like the ancient Maya.

12 Key Dates

2500 BCE
The Preclassic Maya period begins.

1000 BCE
The ancient Maya begin to live in villages.

300–800 CE
The Classic period in ancient Maya civilization.

511–527 CE
Lady of Tikal rules over the city-state of Tikal.

583–604 CE
Lady Yohl Ik'nal rules over the city-state of Palenque.

600 CE
The population of a Maya city-state in modern-day Belize reaches one million.

1200 CE
Chichén Itzá, Mayapán, and Izamal are powerful cities in Mexico.

1502 CE
Spanish soldiers make contact with the ancient Maya.

1697 CE
The last ancient Maya city is destroyed by the Spanish.

1703 CE
A Spanish religious leader finds a surviving copy of the *Popol Vuh*.

1830s CE
American John Lloyd Stephens finds Maya ruins and writes books about his findings.

1952 CE
Yuri Knorosov realizes that Maya hieroglyphics represent speech sounds.

Glossary

alliance
An agreement of organizations to work together.

ancestor
Someone from whom a person or group came.

ancient
Belonging to a period long ago.

archaeologist
A person who studies past human life by examining things left by ancient peoples.

civilization
The way of life of a people.

culture
The beliefs and characteristics of a group of people.

drought
A long period of dry weather.

hieroglyphics
A way of writing that uses pictures to represent words.

maize
Corn.

reservoir
A human-made place where water is stored.

For More Information

Books

Doeden, Matt. *Tools and Treasures of the Ancient Maya.* Minneapolis: Lerner Publications, 2014.

Hunter, Nick. *Daily Life in the Maya Civilization.* Chicago: Heinemann Raintree, 2016.

Somervill, Barbara A. *Ancient Maya.* New York: Children's Press, 2013.

Tieck, Sarah. *Maya.* Minneapolis, MN: Abdo Publishing, 2015.

Visit 12StoryLibrary.com

Scan the code or use your school's login at **12StoryLibrary.com** for recent updates about this topic and a full digital version of this book. Enjoy free access to:

- Digital ebook
- Breaking news updates
- Live content feeds
- Videos, interactive maps, and graphics
- Additional web resources

Note to educators: Visit 12StoryLibrary.com/register to sign up for free premium website access. Enjoy live content plus a full digital version of every 12-Story Library book you own for every student at your school.

Index

About the Author

Elaine A. Kule has taught reading and writing to elementary-age students. She has also written books and short works for children.